The Time Change

The Time Change

poems by

Lynne Hugo deCourcy

&

Ampersand Press/Bristol, RI

Acknowledgements

Grateful acknowledgement is made to the editors of the following magazines in which these poems first appeared:
Calliope: "Dancing to Glenn Miller," "June First," "His Good Life," "Visiting the Graves"
Calyx: "The Task at Hand"
Cincinnati Poetry Review: "Autumn Drive"
The Devil's Millhopper: "War Baby"
Embers: "Affirmation," "What I Have," "Passing through Darrville"
Great River Review: "Evening Prayer"
G.W. Review: "Winter Storm"
Kalliope: "Fear"
Mid-America Review: "The Pearls," "Changing the Gown"
Negative Capability: "Recognition"
The New Laurel Review: "The Dancing Dream"
Poets On: "Bearing Comfort"
The Quarterly: "Escape," "Sister, Did You Used to Pray," "Watching My Daughter Skate: In Training," "Traveling," "Like Any Woman: Those Dreams," "The Life of the Writer," "Reunion with White Zinfandel"
Prairie Schooner: "At Bedtime"
South Florida Poetry Review: "Afterlife"
Tar River Poetry: "Truce"
Three Rivers Poetry Journal: "Taking Him from the Cell"
The Wisconsin Review: "Fire," "In Florida," "Clarity"
Zone 3: "The Good Child," "Apology," "Exposure"

Some of these poems also appeared in a chapbook, *The Good Child*, published by Still Waters Press, 1990.

My thanks to the Ohio Arts Council, The Kentucky Foundation for Women, and the National Endowment for the Arts for generous grants while this work was in progress and warm appreciation to Martha Christina of Ampersand Press. Special thanks to Scott Jackson for the cover painting, "The Time Change."

composition and design by Ampersand Press

Library of Congress Catalog Card Number: 91-73699
ISBN 0-935331-13-1

first printing June 1992

Printed in U.S.A.
Recycled paper and soy ink

Published by Ampersand Press
Creative Writing Program
Roger Williams College
Bristol, RI 02809

In memory of Lora Atherton Hugo

> *And still...I sway like one fainting strand*
> *Of spiderweb, glittering and vanishing and frail*
> *Above the river.*
>
> —James Wright

and for my family

Contents

I

Question

I know your fear,
your history coming for you,
but can you not turn
and say welcome,
even if her coming were to scatter
the polished shells of your several
lives, displayed, but as empty
as the years of your absence?
Can you not let them
go, and open your arms
to the grace of a
coherent life? The child
you left has grown, and now she swims
toward your island, she swims
up in your dreams
as though from the obscure
ocean floor. At first,
her spreading hair hides
her head, but it flows
back as she rises
more quickly,
until you recognize the pearls
around her neck, until
at once she breaks the glassy
surface of your life, her
clear face a reflection of your own
before you gave up
what you believed.
Can you not let everything else
go, and say welcome?

Staring Down the Distance

Korea was nowhere I'd heard of
but I knew my father had come home
in '46 wanting sons
and that nothing was where
it was supposed to be;
he'd had two daughters
and now his unit could be called up again
any old time,
so he went to the range every week
to shoot 45s at printed outlines of
the faceless, sexless, unyielding;
torn open with holes
they hung there, unmoved.
Like an unkillable despair
they hung there, while he shot again
and again, open-eyed and unflinching.

Some nights he took me with him;
he taught me to shoot
like a son with the men
and I tried to follow him
into the length of dead
silence he heard in his mind,
to make unflinching holes in the heart
of the target.
I rounded my eyes into glassy
unblinking moons, staring down the distance,
to absorb the kick that shuddered
through my body with every explosion,
the bang of beginnings
and the bang of endings
when I was ten
sounding all the same to me.

War Baby

Once each summer our father took us
to Playland in Rye, New York,
where my sister and I had our fortunes
told by gypsies, their long red fingernails
curling over our palms in their hands
and heads bent over our futures,
but none of them said the same thing,
nothing you could count on, and I
added this to my list of bad signs,
like the absence of the words
or touch from him
that might have freed me.

I blamed the war and how the bad talk never
stopped, but maybe
I had lost him to something else entirely;
there were only furtive evil maybes
floating like specks in front of my eyes,
bad signs every one, and I was afraid to ride
the ferris wheel turning like years
to hurdy-gurdy music
in front of us all night.

But my sister was not the kind to see
danger; she'd wear me down
until finally I'd climb on with her,
our father waiting on the ground,
a *Pall Mall* hanging from his bottom lip,
in the shadows like something
you could lose sight of in an instant
if the wheel stopped with us swaying
at the top of July
and you threw back your head and laughed
as though there were no need to worry,

or you looked around to love the world
spread below, lit, and filled with
tinny music,
                    or straight up
to love the wide, mysterious sky
where the air thinned, cool and starry;
I wanted to look everywhere
and breathe it all in
like a life I could have
but I had learned the fear of
love, the way a mother never feels safe
her eyes off her first baby, knowing
that so much love is doom
and when we stopped at the top
I kept my eyes on the spot
where I thought he was
while I clutched the bar and willed the wheel
down to the ground where I could see him.

Dancing to Glenn Miller

The room was beige in the fashion
of the fifties but my father
still believed in Glenn Miller,

told me "*This* is music,"
swaying, his feet and hips
and shoulders moving like smooth

oiled parts. My feet were in white
anklets when he set them on top
of his polished black shoes,

and when my body tried to lie
to please him, he barked "just *listen*,
don't *think*." Later I learned

to move like a mirror with him
and he liked me if I didn't
stumble; then he would close his eyes

and lips and hum from another place.
Sometimes the closest someone can get
to love is dipping sowly

to a long note shuddering to a
thin sad end, when the clarinet
is a falling star.

Escape

She'd taken one of her fits that day,
our Mother, dragging the furniture
out as curbside trash
until there was no sign
of a made life that might hold
a person in place,
until the living room was
only a couch where she slept away
from us, ghostly,
like a dampness you might reach
through, and we held our arms
crossed, hands tucked under,
our mouths quiet as cotton.
But one of us made noise
once, or touched; the frame
of the couch cracked,
roused our Mother to a loud
thick labor, dragging it
to the back yard
where it rained until that couch
half-floated, half-sank,
and then faded in the sun
like an abandoned rowboat hopelessly
waiting for rescue.
That year, after every new rain,
my sister swore she'd dreamed
of oars and
begged me to help her find them.

Fire

The earth was soft
beneath my knees and the grass
swarmy with new ants when I crouched
over a dry, brown leaf, its points curled in
like fingers over an empty palm,
my own hand above it holding
a magnifying glass at a slant
to pull sun from the sky.
I'd heard at school
you could make fire that way.

The earth, still wet, was seeping
through my pants; how impossible seemed fire,
how far away the summer, life starting to rustle
and buzz and creep but slowly, too
slowly; and I was
about to give up when smoke curled
like a beckoning finger, a single thin wisp
rising like yes! just before

the leaf arched and flamed and I leapt
to stamp it out, as though I could
stamp out the terror of anything
I started in the world,
as though I could
stamp out the fires of hand and heart
to come, love
leaping from my fingertips and
spreading out of control.

The Dancing Dream

In a dream I danced
with a stranger
in a frescoed ballroom,
domed like the sky.
It was music I breathed;
then I was music
and flowed into him, like
stream into river,
river into sea.
It was not the applause I
mourned when I woke
(nor the press of my breasts on his chest)
but the loss of that perfect knowing:
where to put my feet,
what to say.

II

Sister, Did You Used to Pray?

Sister,
did you used to pray in your secret bed,
knees drawn up and wrapped
in your own arms, did you ever
pray to be different tomorrow,
sure-footed and smart and pretty,
like the hand of God had finally picked you?
And the next day by noon
some blonde girl named Caroline
or Gloria, or a paradise like Angela,
would be first again, lacy and bowed
in a sundress on the swing,
singing all the words
to a song you didn't know. And
like a stone you would still be squat
and dull on the earth, while
God was something filmy
someone else could swing to
for Him to pick her again
and again for the dance.
Now, sister, if this despair was
ever yours, I believe you will know
how I pray for my daughter Angela
all the while I iron her dresses and push
the swing; I believe you will know
how fierce this tie double-knotted by pain,
how terrible this love; I believe
you will understand that, even knowing better,
I make her learn the words
to every song I ever heard
the angels sing.

Fear

I am pale
enough to be invisible here,
so intense this gathering
of light. I draw my legs up
on the small white towel
to avoid the burning sand,
knowing I can watch unnoticed
that sleek boy, so dark
and white-toothed he must
have been born in the sun,
sure how to wear
his smooth-muscled shoulders.
It has been years, still

I feel a stirring
and, as though it were casual,
I mold my hands around
my own waist, remembering
the day when a boy
with a new license took me
to the beach and oiled my back.
His hands were slippery and hot
when he lifted me over his head
in the waist-deep murky water
where I could not see the bottom.
My breasts were small and my legs
ungainly, pink and white as a crab's
scurrying back to the sandy shallows
for a place to hide.

I remember how fear won then
and today I have no idea
what I wish, though this boy
is my son and long at home

in the deep water, head-first
diving, leaving me
only glimpses of an arching body
rippling among the waves until
what must come: he lifts

a copper-glinting girl by her waist
above his head. Her heavy breasts
spilling from their cups
show the white line where
their secrets begin,
like a soft underbelly.
But she makes no move
to fix the suit; instead she squeals
and tips her body forward
on the fulcrum of his hands
until her breasts, hardly contained
at all, sway
just above my son's mouth
which is open, laughing.

June First

June first, fat and ripe with sun as
the strawberries lying on warm earth, waiting
tooth-ready with juice;
the sprinkler flings dazzling arcs into the
light and my daughter plays on the grass
three days before the end of school,
the summer spread before her like a feast.
She prances, teasing herself with the
sprinkler on the first hot, still day, her
bright-striped suit glistening taut and sleek,
and, I am not ready for this, I see
the faintest rising across her chest,
like a suggestion of hills hardly discernible
on the horizon.
But today is just the first, still early,
she is not 10 yet, and she plays and shrieks,
the arc of flashing drops chasing her,
"help me! save me!"
loving the thrill of danger.
The day seems so benignly kind, with
evil napping in some dark thicket far
from this groomed lawn sparkling with
light and water, that I take the risk,
I have to start sometime,
I raise cool clean water into the
light like her life in my hands, and
tossing it into the air, I call back
"save yourself!"

His Good Life

We are lurching toward eighteen
with this child, the first, the son
who was born flailing like a boxer
and hardly ever hears
a bell ending rounds. He dances
around us, feinting, ducking;
he has not decided yet
how he's going to turn out
and we are always fighting him
for the slippery chance of his good
life.
His body is wiry, too hard to hold
sorrow yet, and slender
enough to slip sideways through
the casement window of his room.
He escapes us, restlessly dozing
on nights like these,
into a car
waiting for him beneath a ripe, full moon
that seems to hang heavy on a fragile thread
like his good life
looking like it could fall down and break
forever on a night so warm and alive
that nothing can be fixed in place.

Taking Him from the Cell

What is hope if not futility
for moments stood on end?
                    Sydney Lea

My son has spent two hours locked
in a cell, sitting, my son,
who has spent two years walking
away, an angry slouching walk,
shoulders hunched over something coiled
inside him, a walk to warn you
the coiled thing is sleeping, but fitfully,
ready to wake and spring.

It is a holding cell, down a long
dim corridor, the distance between worlds,
behind a rectangle of wired window, stark
and unflinching as his eyes have grown,
a cement cell with one wooden
bench where a boy caught drinking
in a car waits; he waits
as long as it takes a mother
or a father to arrive; and

I have taken my time. I want him
broken, as I am broken to the bit
of failure; its metallic taste on my tongue.
I want the coiled creature he keeps
inside defeated, crawling out of my son
on its belly, leaving his body pliant,
willing, as it used to be. I want him
small again, held in the cell of my body;
I want to start over.

I want this until I see him there, broken, small,
his length of legs beneath him in a huddle,
nails bitten lower than the
soft quick, bleeding at the edges
on hands that swipe at his face;
I hear the rough sobs of the small
son who cried, surrounded by my arms,
when love was a white thread
I could follow, the straight line from
the intention of my heart

to what became of it.
I circle an arm around his back while
I sign my name to take him out,
from the cell into the world,
starting again, knowing nothing
I can change, everything here
futile, upended into hope.

At Bedtime

When we read together, my daughter breaks off
to read something funny aloud. Then she goes
on, she tells me about the riverboats
on the Ohio, what Kyle said, and how she always
ends up sitting beside some dumb
boy. She wants to skate in the Olympics, she wants
her dog to stay healthy, she needs
a ten speed bike.
               When she is back to her book
I sneak enough looking to trace my tall family
tree growing up from the length of her big
toes, legs, waist, fingers—those definite
genes. And the way she wants no one ever
angry; her feelings, bruisable as soft
fruit: there is my own self.
               It is the separate
way she marks her own place, like the strange
contained strength of how silently she pushes
herself into the cold air of fear
unwarmed by words, that is
different from me as her fine sheer
blondeness,
           and tonight I think that after all
it will be what is not me in her that saves
her in the end.

While she falls alseep, her breath
spreads across the pillow like a deft
hand smoothing a path through wrinkles, with
steady strokes, sure as something to
believe in. I lie with her, her back
nested into my front
and I match her breath
           for breath

long and even, in and out by
turns, indivisible halves of supplication
and praise for the me and the not me
of her; I breathe in please and
thank you I breathe out.

The Good Child

For years, perhaps, my good child has hidden
scraps of frustration, like ends of red yarn
rolled into a ball.

This child, the one whose best defense is no offense,
who quietly pulls the stinger of her brother's insults
from her flesh,
whose desires are so simple,
whose quick gratitude for small favors lays down balm
like a brushful of clear yellow light across my mind,

this girl has not forgotten anything; she has not forgotten
how a speeding van killed her dog,
how the new girl in the neighborhood took away
her best friend,
the times she's given in,
the times I've not been there,
or been there too much;

tonight she unravels the ball into a great raging
tantrum; she stands and screams
unreasoning as cement, immovable
until there is nothing for me to do but lift her,
arms and legs flailing like the frayed
ends of exposed nerves,
and stagger with her to her room.
Strands of blonde hair fly loose around her head
like dandelion fluff in a storm, seeds
of anger scattering to plant themselves
in the dirtiest corners of the house

to grow up, while in her bedroom
crumpled tissues will litter the bed and floor,
and the first "I hate you"

can be practiced, silently rolling
around inside her mouth like stones
over the flint of her tongue
until they spark
and she can spit the flaming words,
the beginning of the fire song
of coming out, of leaving.

Watching My Daughter Skate: In Training

for Brooke

Here is what I must do
in the space between heartbeats
when her body is an
upthrust of wings:
release her. In the spinning
moment, fragile as my bones
and hers, when everything
I love is mortal
and gleaming,
let her go;
let the thin ice of my
heart crack from
the weight of watching;
I am in training to sleep
beneath a sky that changes
night by night of
its own accord,
let the white stars stay
up or fall without me.

III

What I Have

Listen! I have this:
an hour I was pure
and time obliged me,
a great red sun hovering
above water, neither rising
nor setting, immense
and still. At the end
of a dock, a man
with our child watching
bright ribbons of sails barely
moving, so calm were
the water and land and
sky, fear not rustling
anywhere. I watched them
watching the boats, tiny fish
leaving slight ripples
around their feet, dangling
in the vast water,
silver and easy as the few
words rippling the air between them,
and I—
I was the open hand of water staying
open, waiting forever,
I was the other hand, the earth
that held them open-palmed,
I was the eye of sky
that watched them and loved them
and wanted nothing else.

The Pearls

I wear my children as any woman does,
like pearls for which I dove
beyond my depth
until I broke the surface gasping,
clutching another beauty,

to be strung, with the others,
into a circle where they stay
fastened against the soft hollow
of my throat

except for a few nights
when my body as it is
is enough for someone,
even for me,
and I reach back to the clasp
which has jagged little serpent
teeth, like something
you might fight to undo.

Like Any Woman: Those Dreams

Like any woman, I have those dreams
of swinging my headlights a half-moon
away from the house. Last night
I dreamed the rain
and the fog mirrored the lights back
and I forgot not to blink,
not to flinch a look
over my shoulder, where

they stood, where they always stand,
behind the glass door
hands and faces pressed there,
silent and moist as roses. Their lips
were set like cracks across
the glass but the rain
slid down their faces in murmurs
(*we know you, we own you*)

in streams, eroding me
like the flow of blood
and love, or something like it,
the murmur I hear like rain:
we know you. We own you.

Winter Storm

for Martha Christina

I begin this poem while I languish in jail
and my husband in the form of an iron
thinks he's hot and cackles at me
from Pennsylvania Avenue, his true colors
flying high. I vow to destroy him
as soon as I'm free; I'll buy the electric company
and be in control of heat and light forever.
My daughter, the banker, clucks in quiet sympathy,
rolls doubles and buys a hotel
with no fanfare, while my son rails; this storm
was clearly arranged to ruin his life, beginning
and beginning to grapple with power.
                                      Their faces
are luminous, separate candles
holding back the black, cold air.
Beyond these candles, the world
is a falling frozen sky,
fragments of dead stars slamming
into the window panes, walls and roof barely holding
back the ice encasing the house, driven into every detail
of lock and latch and crack by the wild
wind that cut loose the electric lines,
toppling poles and snapping trees.

Candlelit, cocooned in double sweatshirts, we huddle
around the board and dice, shaking
our futures, like a glowing heart beating
inside the ice of the end of the earth,
each of us being our
                              selves and one I
of us, inextinguishable
as mirth in the house of mourning, the fire
inside the ice burning on, still burning.

Clarity

The small pond we found before
we find again, this time with none
of August's heady overgrowth blurring the edges

of water into weed and field and wood,
or its thick heat lowering the pond
to a murky, rancid green; it is high now

and transparent, the whole clearing
distinct as early April,
sharp, separate cattails outlined by

sky and the split pods of milkweed
still holding their filmy seed
in fragile, clinging cascades. Small touches

of greening, a piercing clarity of blue.
Above, two hawks circle
dipping, rising, with unmoving wings

stretched full-open, riding the thermals.
I want to stop, to forget every
name, every date and task,

to be above the clearing
on those unflurried wings, seeing
the narrow planes of your long body,

the mysterious hesitations
of my hands and heart, always
holding back, wanting

something else. What? The dog strains
on the leash, front legs pawing the air.
You move and I am drawn on the moving

earth, before I can be still, before
I can see where I am heading,
going on, gaining or losing ground,

toward the spreading roots and clinging arms
of summer, the choking proliferation
that I will try to love.

The Life of the Writer

You should see me
with this paring knife,
dividing grapefruit sections.
But surely it is good
to make breakfast
even when it means the fruit
gets cut in half and then
divided with an inadequate tool
into tiny separate sections,
each cut leaving some behind,
the rest spooned out and
gone, before I can even picture the whole
yellow-pink roundness forming
like a small early sun
in silent, fragrant air, gathering into itself
a full measure of juice, somewhere
in a distant orchard long before
it was divided and divided
and divided.

Passing through Darrville

On Route 127, slim ribbon woven through land
frosted by the bleached remains of the corn crop,
randomly dotted with isolated farms,
         a blink
a town like a cluster of blooms somewhere
in a vast field.
     Don's Carry Out,
       The Hitching Post: a string of white
lights outline the one window like stars,
leaves the yellow moon to the *Miller Highlife* sign.
Pickup trucks are lined
outside like faithful animals napping
while they wait.
      A few houses,
sagging porches edging the curbless street,
someone's home, someone's sprung trap,
like none other,
like any other.
       One way ticket take me anywhere—
      northbound, southbound, I don't even care
Mama Cass sings as though the radio came
from the future instead of a time
as full of dead ends as cold stars if
that's the way you think when you glance up.
Not that I think of that, it's just natural
how my foot weighs itself on the gas while I sing with her,
passing through everywhere I've been
and wanted to leave, everywhere
        I ever wanted to go.

Reunion, with White Zinfandel

for Susan M. Petrie

Look what I have brought you:
the grape skins were left in
just long enough to raise
the faintest blush in the wine,
like a bottle of an unopened dawn,
or a swan eye that remembers us

in the suburbs at eighteen,
our necks fragile and curving
in the early blush of time,
waiting on the station platform
for the New York train
that would take us away.

After my car has spilled
the litter of miles, the children will
spar and laugh through dinner until
finally, we fold them away
and open the bottle. I will swear
your eyes are no different now;
I will swear we still have time.

In the late cold hours
we will each climb drunkenly
into the beds where
husbands of twenty years snore.
Our coming will stir the sheets
of their sleep to a jagged man-breathing,
but I, for one, will lie
stone quiet until he is still again,

and run my hands up

and down my body,
thinking it's not so different
as it was. I will wait
on this platform for a train
even as soberness overtakes me,
even as I know
the children will call me
in the first blush light
of their day.

Apology

Fourth grade, that year when the chrysalis just begins
to split and I talk more,
and more intently, to my daughter,
a study in shining symmetry
and light, I talk to her
about cruelty, wanting her spared
the scars cruelty leaves,
like the one I found tonight,
remembering you, Bert, struggling to raise
your name from beneath thirty years:

Albert Bertram. Bert, that name I spoke
with such disgust and loathing,
even then knowing the cruelty of it,
but laying that name like balm over my flaws,
relieved that I could never be so ugly as you
with that nose, flat and squashed to the side
as though perpetually against an invisible window,
watching the classroom through it,
watching the playground through it,
a long scar down one side crossed with the tracks
of old stitching, like a railroad line going nowhere.

Bert, I pray you are whole now and healed,
sleeping at this moment by a woman
whose arm is laid across your back
while she listens to you breathe
and gives thanks that all
your suffering was a line to bring you there,
your face loved even in your sleep,
having long forgiven us, your debtors,
bearing our scars.

Bearing Comfort

My friend's husband will die soon.
On the pillow is the puffed
gray mushroom of his face, his
hand fluttering now and then
like the papery points of decayed leaves.
There is a no in this room
to replace every yes that was, every yes
I will, yes I can, and what remains
seems only plaintive: her hair is still
a lush chestnut when she stands up
by the tall separateness of their sons.

She tells me that in this bedroom they papered
in green, even with people always lining the
walls like a parade route, the flowered bed
the main float, she thinks of cradling
his shrunken sex in her hands, of closing
her mouth around it fiercely until
it comes back to life and she can fill
the empty place inside her with it and move
her body over him again and
again until she drives him, wills him,
forces him to find a future
in his own body and send it out, rejoicing.

She tells me this and I want to cradle
her head against my own breast
with my hands, my hands that will
guide a husband into me tonight.
I want to cradle her head
in false comfort to stifle her words;
what I want to hear is
what will let me live.

Autumn Drive

Late October's late afternoon
cold and the sky's quick sinking,
its light flaming across the tops
of trees before it drops behind
the hills and the black trunks press
hard into the land. The cattle are still
grazing, though, and for a moment I think
there is still time
and light left. The road winds
ahead until it curves out of sight,

and the rear view is of years
and years of autumn dusks, my blood
stirring restless as leaves
as daily the earth changes,
moving on, and somehow I have missed it
again: some grasp,

some knowing, just eluding me
about the peace at the center of
this flux: a sad, brave peace holding
its own place like the wooden stakes hammered
toward the heart of the earth
that yesterday held signs
exhorting my vote for this, against that,
now standing empty as a leafless tree,
their answer lost overnight to wind and rain
as though it's all been settled
before I decided anything.

IV

The Time Change: October

I could live
forever here in trailless woods
retrieving everything that smacks of endings
for a defiant bouquet. Even now,
a notion of time,
     one afternoon,
        can be set
around to endlessness. Gathering milkweed
with suede pods spilling filmy futures,
resilient cattails, bittersweet
wrapped in thorny bushes, finally opening
the tough casings around their red hearts—
and a crown of sumac—
      I could believe
these deep leaves a bed
where, if I slept,
     it would not matter,
time not advancing, but opening
into itself.
    I could believe myself all the way
back and ahead,
my mother's mother,
     and child,
       my child
        and hers
body after perfect
body all eclipsed into
one, here,
carrying this bouquet
wearing this crown.

Truce

> *Truce, this instant, with what's to come.*
> Maxine Kumin

Across the lake, the hills,
low trees and brush
blazing in the sun, the high white poplar
already blown bare and poking skyward
like the masts of the boats
being winter-readied all month.
                                But today
everyone is forgiving a warm world
for the hardships ahead: young men lie
in the grass,
                    shirtless, their shoulders
curved and hard as their frisbees.
A girl feeds mallards, the males' heads iridescent
green as summer flies,
                        quiet for once,
and content as the circle of their white necklaces
in the plenty of the bread on the water.
A wasp nest, abandoned
into light
and lightness, dangles like a huge
scalloped pine cone, suspended
in the space between the heartbeats
of danger
            and beauty.
For a time I believe
                        I have arrived
wherever I was going. The moment stretches

beyond the boundaries of its rightful life
then snaps back on the elastic sound
of a motorboat

                    starting up the great hum
of the spinning earth
again, gunning the afternoon
towards what's to come:
                              an early night,
winter.

Balancing Act

Extending our ache of shoulder by long-armed poles
with stiff fingers, we have raked
this yard down the waning light
toward the porch, where the lamp is
lit. We climb the few steps
to rest and balance on the rail, talking
while evening advances on the leaves
in rounded piles, ready to be bagged.
Crickets rattle their slow deaths and we take
the comfort of familiar songs. The dogs curl
in tail-to-nose circles, and sigh.
A chancey wind
                anytime now
would undo the whole effort of gathering
what forces beyond us have scattered.
Still, we perch here in the land
of strange faiths, where
moths are throwing themselves at the light
like white-robed monks, burning themselves
alive in urgent warning about something,
while nearby, peaceable kingdoms turn themselves around
a few times, choosing a comfortable spot
before lying down to dream.

Entering Manhood

The length of my son is folded in,
like bent stems and petals
on the blue-flowered sheets in his room, where
walls and ceilings hold taped-up
posters of red coupes, with
long female legs on bodies with breasts,
lips, and polished, sculpted nails,
poised by the car door, ready
for him, jazz playing for him
as he takes his place on the long
open road.
                        A night ago he lay
on red flowers of broken glass
with a girl, one with chewed-off nails,
whose stubby legs bent the wrong way beneath her
while he moved on top of her in a parody
of what he'd imagined a hundred times,
lying on those blue-flowered sheets.
His floor is spread with yellow citations
like a fall garden flung to disarray by the crash,
a bouquet mixed with the paper details
of other wrong turns,
                        as though he has had his face
pressed to that glass, like a child looking out
at the road he would drive down in
red coupes, with long-haired, Obsession-scented
girls,

                        and the glass has already begun to break,
the way glass breaks and breaks
into fragments too small to ever piece
back together
and the effort cuts your fingers; oh god,
how the hopeless effort cuts you.

Exposure

Even this morning,
snow-covered, the bent stems of
impatiens still spill color. Red salvia,
geraniums, roses
that have spent a week answering the
leaves' mounting challenge with the intensity
of accumulated summer, all stand
like something bloody and doomed.

I go out to shake the dense weight
from laden branches. An elm broke
in the wild, unreasonable night;
it lies in disarray on unharvested
squash, pumpkins, the bitten
finish of tomatoes.
Unmittened, my fingers chip away
the ice gloved on the buds of flowers
(as though they might yet open). Angry
at everything unsavable,
                        I go in,
remove wet shoes, wet socks.
My narrow ankles and feet
poke from the raw flaps of pants—
how like pale branches they look,
naked,
all their frail veins bared.

The Task at Hand

for David

The time change has somehow taken us
by surprise: still early, it is night
enough that my son and I can barely see
each other as we pull out the remains
of the flower garden. Each of us ruthlessly
pushes aside foliage (some still green,
I remember, though the hour browns it all,
stiffening my resolve like whiskey)
and goes for the plant's anchor.
We grasp summer-thick stems with both hands,
and, knees bent for leverage,
uproot each bushy plant, yank out
the deep tentacles extended
toward the cupped palm of the earth.

We are arguing again, though not about
the task at hand; clearing
this space is mindless, requiring only the blind
strength to rip out what's grown here, even
the last marigolds with their
fragile casings of winged seeds.
The earth and roots cling to one another
as they split,
                            that tearing noise
marks the steady rhythm of our work
as we are uprooting, arguing, uprooting.

V

Recognition

I saw a stranger's face through his windshield
and mine, hazed like two decades, and it was my father,
my father as I still see him,
not the arthritic man, jowled and sallow-skinned
whose beard, gray-white as the end
of a burned-out match, waits for noon
or a reason to shave,
who has nothing to say, no more
curses and no words to recall the old ones.

There, in that car at the stop sign, was the groomed man
who'd gone on the road making hearty sales calls,
calling the buyers you horse's ass, you
and making them love it, love him,
making everyone love him and I
loved him even when I hated him most,
when he'd say I was a nothing, just
a nothing and his indifference to me
was massive and killing as his chest
sucking all the air from a room.

I saw that man and I wanted
to jump from my own car, the Buick
I'd thought would impress him,
and run through the August heat rising wavy and thick
as pain off the road,
run in my high heels and suit to that man,
my poems crammed alive, like flowers,
into a briefcase banging against my thigh,
petals of paper poking between the hinges—
waving diplomas, waving my vita,
pictures of my children under each arm,
I wanted to run across the gravel scattered
on the scarred road, though my heels would sink

in the melting tar and trip me,

I wanted to make it
across the road like time,
across time like an oozing, unhealed wound;
I wanted to run to that man and cry Daddy!
I, my own woman,
my husband's woman, my children's mother,
just wanted to be his girl and run to him and cry
look Daddy, something! I am something!
and wait there, blocking his way, melting, sinking,
sweating, until I heard him say yes.

In Florida

On the boulevard where he lives now
royal palms dust the sky, wispy-haired and
spindly as life on a single leg
that any good wind could snap.
        'Tis the season
my father says, balefully opening mail,
liver-spotted hands unfolding news of sickness
and death: his friends, their wives,
even their daughters and sons, he adds,
his hooded eyes casting an afternoon shadow
over me before he goes to his nap
          and I to a walk
on the beach, heading north by habit
and by longing.
Today the tide is full high
and strong at two, rolling in wave
after wave as it always has
and light glints on the water
as though I could follow it
        all the way back
to when today was the future, unreal
as any future, and then
was all there was.
He never changed year
       to year
before he moved here
and today I set an escape pace, I want
to walk all the way back
to where forever was,
where surely I could still find him
         home
scorning help from the young dumb likes
of me, shingling a roof, remote and
single-handed as God.

                    I stretch the thought
as though it were a piece of dune grass held
between my thumbs that I could blow
into a semblance of a remembered tune
and walk on,
lured by the surf always pulling back
like hands teasing out hope just ahead,

until I am exhausted
and the iridescent green-backed flies are biting,
stinging little jabs of the present.
                              I turn around
to see how the sky has thickened behind me,
late clouds hiding the point of change, sky
to sea, afternoon to evening.
For a moment
                  this
seems all there is, the past lost again
and the future as unreal as any future,
but the surf has quieted all the way down
and plays weakly, the tide having turned
imperceptibly into a minor key.

Evening Prayer

As I lie down to sleep,
unfold the covers in an amber
circle of bedside light,
the wrinkled hand with ridged nails
that lifts the sheet hardly seems my own,
but my Mother's, when she was
already old, straightening the sheets
around me, stroking my back
in the apple-green room that was mine.

Back turned from the light and
face half to pillow, you sleep
chest rising in small sighs
for something just out of reach—
like the plaintive mews we heard
in the childrens' room, when by
nightlight we watched the
dreams flicker on their faces,
as I watch yours now

and notice your hair more gray,
like my Father's, when he was
already old. I consider this
and use my roughened hand
to stroke your back, write on it
with a ridge-nailed finger through
the cotton across your back,
what I want you to know
if I should die before I wake.

Changing the Gown

I was a long time being born as
you are a long time dying,
lingering impossibly past
learned predictions by men
who didn't know us well enough,
postponing our journeys.
When I change your gown made wet
by life oozing away,
you curl to a primal pose
against the chill,
the same pose I must once
have held, knees to chin,
clinging to the safe warmth in you.
Was I afraid then to come out
as you are afraid now to go back in?
You hold my finger in the reflexive grip
of the newborn and the dying,
my arm like an umbilical cord
to hold you here,
against a second severing.
Oh Mother, how you and I hate
lightless tunnels, uncertain destinations.
Now amniotic waters bathe you again
and the sheets cocoon your body
as it shrinks into itself.
Your fever eyes look beyond me
to burn a path in the dark.

What Might Happen at Your Mother's Grave

It might be in New Jersey, whole stories
that are not stories are often set in New Jersey
in a ramshackle suburb outside
a place like Newark.
Near the cemetery, the freeway
ramp might arch like a drained rainbow
and the groan and rumble of freight may
drown what you'd played out in your mind
during the long dying, imagining this first visit
back: some sweetness of stirring leaves, a bird
calling like an old notion of peace.
What you might find could make you
crazy: that noise
of moving trucks carrying loads
that put you in mind of some unfinishable
wasted task,
mossy, unkempt graves, the stones choking
on weeds the way even the most mundane
unlovely life is enough to overrun memory;

and then you might find that her name—
carved beneath his on her husband's stone,
there thirty years already—
is completely covered by the ragged brown
leaves and grayed paper refuse
piled there by an oily prevailing wind.
Her name
is covered as completely
as though she'd never been,
even the years of birth and death are covered,
and in some rage like a fanned despair
you might dig with your manicured hands,
scoop up scraps and leaves
and the remains of the last summer

and fling them aside, to clear
the earth away from her name,

as though the point
of her life came down to her name.
Maybe you even look at your own hands
as they trace the letters you've revealed,
caressing the O
with tenderness, anger, apology
as though it were the oval of her face
you wouldn't touch for years;
maybe you look at the living flesh
of your two hands,
but there is no way you will settle
for that, even if you are a woman
yourself with a daughter,
there is no way you will settle
so small, you know it has to stop
somewhere,
you go to find the cemetery keeper:
you want that stone set again, higher.

Visiting the Graves

for Jeffrey

When I was a child, the cemetery was small,
like a few scattered buildings in a country
town, surrounded by fields,
but year by year, it fills
and widens—
a tenement now, thousands of mismatched
stones with weeds between concrete,
a miniature city of the dead sprawling
to join the city of the living,
spreading in turn to meet it.

One by one, my family moves
across the blurring line
and those left alive make our erratic
visits. This time my sister and I
have brought the children;
there is something we want them to know,
though here we are, wordless,
not knowing what to tell them
that matters—not even knowing
what we want ourselves to know.
We look dumbly at the chiseled dates,
the names. So much has come
to only this.

The oldest boy has wandered off;
finally we spot him thirty rows away.
He has found a fresh-dug unfilled grave,
prone shoulders and arms of dirt spread
open, just waiting
for someone. He is jumping
side to side; backing up, he measures

his stride and takes off, exuberant,
leaping like a stag escaping
a clumsy hunter,
and I want him to do what he wants,
I want him to make it, again and again,
while he knows he can easily leap
that puny hole in the ground.
What's the big deal, he says.
It's easy; there's plenty of room to spare.

Affirmation

In the black time
before dawn, frozen in this bed of dozens
of childhoods, huddled beneath layers, my heart is
like a bulb buried inside
the turned earth of my body, rooted here.

This house has held life, attic to cellar, life
has overflowed from the clawfoot tub
on the second floor, slid with eight
children down the worn bannister, and run
through the arched doorways, down
the basement stairs to the coal cellar
where they would hide from their father,
stumbling after them, mean, his cigar
glowing like the furnace door. They ducked
and grew, leaving by turn, still believing
their good mother's stories until he died
of cirrhosis thirty years ago. Everyone came

for his funeral, the house draped in mourning
and joyous with reunions, full, full
of the children and their children. I slept
in the spare room behind the kitchen
with cousins in the bed
our parents had all used one time
or another, coming home from war
or with a new husband, and later
laying us, their own babies, Eskimo-style
in the bed when they came again
for holidays. But that was years
and years ago and now it is his wife
lying upstairs dying and I am alone
in the bed remembering

how it was once and will never be
again, the house crowded with us children
sneaking to see the dungeon downstairs,
hiding from each other in the pantry where
her neat mason jars lined the shelves:
green beans, the bright hearts of tomatoes, pale
translucent pears from the tree
in the small back yard. Mincemeat,
apple and custard, whole tables
of pies at Thanksgiving
and the quiet excuses she made
for us all, as she had for him,
until too many were gone

and she decided to die this year
deep in February while the world is
silent, its crying smothered in snow, and powerless
to warm the few gathered: me and two
of her daughters keeping watch.
The old coal furnace
is long cold, dead as spent passions
and half of her children,
the rest growing old themselves, retiring
to their separate distant ends.

My eyes open to an undeniable
day; filled with the life of all
that has died
and will die, I still
live, I live.

Afterlife

for my father

Like round, mute faces of animals, wary
but wanting,
our knees touch,
                    startle back,
                                touch
while I read to you. I read
the poem of your mother's dying, that long wound
of life oozing out just faster
than water could be dropped,
                                teaspoon
by teaspoon
into the sunken pouch of her cheek.
                                This
is the whole meaning of blood,
of losing, of the chances captives take:
                                I read to you,
let my knees touch yours.

What would I say to you straight out
after so long   and
what would you say back, after all?

Your hair is sparse as whispers now,
barely real, like us together, here;
and I am aging, too.

So are beginning the first small signs
of the afterlife   which will never be enough:
this tentative, grazing touch,
one poem before the silence
of your eyes watering over to brightness
like stones in a stream in the wilderness

of a strange land.

Too soon we will part
for the last time, the lips of our knees
having touched   the most we ever spoke,
the great embrace
ungiven,   the words
that might have died with us
                              living on,
unsaid.

The Next Place

*The hymns and requiems. The sense of movement
as you're borne along to the next place.*
                    Raymond Carver

Airplane, and another in Atlanta
over to the lowcountry coast.
A rental car, passing beneath the woman-
arms of live oaks hung in their exotic
tattered shawls of moss,
to a barrier island,
bicycle over to the far side
one foot after the other until the feet
are in sand
until they are ankle deep in warm
warm water
and there is no place further I can
go,
except the high nest of the osprey, its mess of
wild sticks and grass remaining intact
through seasons,
or the protected place
where loggerhead turtles lay their eggs,
and by law no one is allowed near
with lights or noise
so the babies can be born
alive, ready for their next place,
no matter how foreign or familiar
it will seem.

Nature Lesson

On this island, the live oaks grow
in the maritime forest
just inland from the salt marsh spartina
and watery channels passable
at high tide in a flat-bottomed boat
but happy to maroon you on mud
if you stay too long past the turn.
But let's say you make it through
that first maze, and onto more solid
ground, still sandy though it is.
There they are: the live oaks, covered
with Spanish moss, lacy-gray
and putting you in mind of discarded
shrouds.
Virginia creeper is working its way up
the old, old trunk,
but crusted on the branches is dead-man's
fern. In a dry spell like this, it dies as brittle
and finished as any life that started green
and ended brown.
                But here's the kicker: wait.
You came to the island to learn this
whether you knew it or not. Wait
for a rain and watch the dead-man's fern
turn green; within an hour it will green
as though it had never heard of drought
or death: now, correctly call it resurrection
fern and contemplate the similarity
between this fern and your life;
hasn't it always rained sooner
or later, no matter what you believed?
You made it here and you will make it
to the next place, no matter how dead you seem
in between.

Lynne Hugo deCourcy's poems have been published widely in literary journals, including *Calliope, Passages North, Poets On:, Tar River Poetry* and *Zone 3*. She has received grants from the Kentucky Foundation for Women, the Ohio Arts Council, and the National Endowment for the Arts. She lives with her family in Oxford, Ohio, where she works as a psychotherapist.